BEAD CROCHET BASICS

ready, set, go!

Bead Index
Actual Size

11° Seed Beads

8° Seed Beads

6° Seed Beads

Size 11° Triangle

Size 8° Triangle

Size 5° Triangle

8 Hex

6 Hex

4mm Cube

9 Tri-Cut

Magatama

Dagger

Tips

Beads:

Most projects call for size 11°, size 8°, or size 6° seed beads. Seed beads are round and are available in a wide range of glass colors and finishes. Other bead shapes suitable for bead crochet include 8 hex, 9 tri-cuts, 4mm cube, and triangle.

In addition, faceted beads, daggers, and drop beads add interesting texture. It is possible to crochet with smaller beads than those listed here, but it takes more time and skill. See bead index.

Bead Management:

It is easier to place beads on a textured surface such as a towel or washcloth. The texture keeps beads from running away when you approach them with a needle.

To Prevent Errors when stringing a pattern, make a sample and tape it to your work surface. String 2" or 1 repeat. Wrap tape firmly around the thread 2" from end. Push the beads firmly against tape. Tape again to hold beads in place. Tape this pattern to your work surface and compare as you string the beads for your project. If you have a copy machine available, make a color copy of your bead string, tape it to your work surface. Check each repeat as you string, correct errors as you go.

For Beginners:

To keep beads in a nice spiral circle for the first few rows, place tip of a round shoelace into center of the chained circle of beads as you join the first chain stitch to the last chain stitch. The shoelace tip is not connected to the chain in any way and will be removed (tip first) after the first 4 to 6 rows.

Mary Libby Neiman

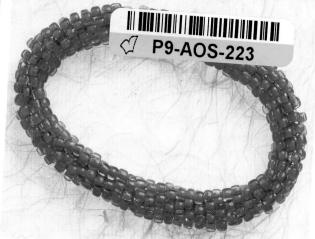

6 beads around

5 beads around

4 beads around

Bead Crochet Basics continued on page 4.

Crochet is fun. Bead crochet is even more fun. Watching a small chain of beads grow into a pretty tubular bracelet is very exciting.

Make a Bobbin

Wind thread and beads on a stiff cardboard bobbin to store your 'inventory'.

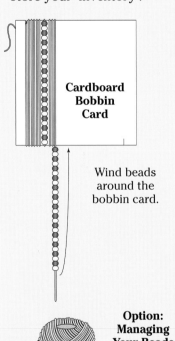

Cardboard Bobbin Card

Wind beads around the bobbin card.

Option: Managing Your Beads

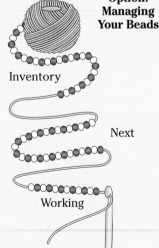

Inventory

Next

Working

Q. Why do I need to make a bobbin?

A. Bead Crochet includes beads in the stitches. Beads are strung onto the thread before any stitches are made and add weight to the thread. It is important to manage this weight so it does not pull too much on the thread or your hand as you work. One way to control this weight is to wind the beaded thread onto a bobbin. Winding a bobbin prevents a tangled mess of beads and wasted thread.

You may want to make more than 1 bobbin. It is difficult to manage more than 2 yards of beads at one time. It is easier to string and crochet 2 yards of beads, stop, cut the working thread, tie the next bobbin thread to your working thread, and continue.

Or add beads to the other end of the thread.

Q. How do I make a bobbin?

A. Cut a 3"-4" square of stiff cardboard. • Measure the thread, adding 10% for error. Insert thread into the eye of a beading needle or thin folded wire. • String the beads in order according to the diagram and push them to the end of the thread.

Wind the beginning of the thread only on a bobbin for 6 turns.

Wind the beads in a ratio of 1/2 turn with beads to 2 1/2 turns thread only. When using a Bead-Slip stitch, this ratio will usually bring up more beads just when you need them.

Begin Bead-Chain stitch - Steps for Blue and White Stripe Bracelet

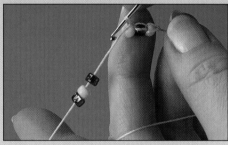

1. Tie a small loop in the end of the thread leaving an 8" tail. Begin the Bead-Chain stitch.

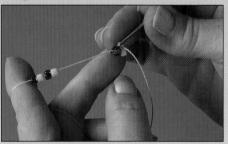

2. Continue Bead-Chain stitch (following the count for your pattern).

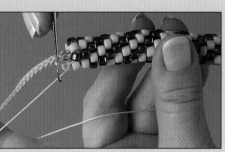

6. Continue to crochet to desired length. Remove shoelace (tip first).

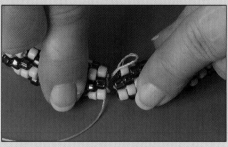

7. Match beads and sew together with the tails of thread.

Joining the beaded chain in a circle with a Bead-Slip stitch

Working Thread

Working thread must be behind and above the next stitch.

1st Bead-Chain stitch

Tail

Slip hook under and bring yarn over to pull a loop through the stitch.

Position of Beads

Beads that have not been stitched stand in a vertical position.

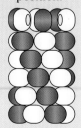

Stitched beads will lie down in a horizontal position.

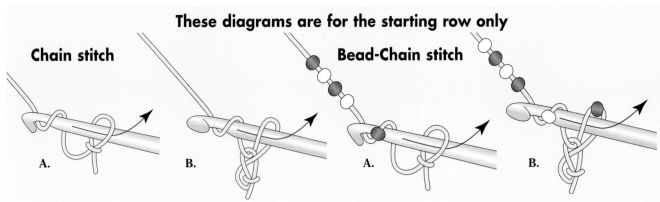

These diagrams are for the starting row only

Chain stitch

A.

B.

Bead-Chain stitch

A.

B.

Bead crochet is easier to learn if you already know how to crochet. If you have not learned to crochet yet, practice the basic stitches using a #2 or #3 steel hook and a #8 or #5 perle cotton thread or Conso thread.

More information on learning to crochet is available on the craft yarn council website at www.learntocrochet.com.

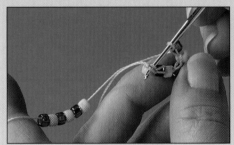

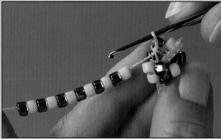

3. Join the beaded chain into a circle (see enlarged diagram on page 4).

4. Insert a shoelace tip into the beaded circle to help maintain the tube shape.

5. Work a Bead-Slip stitch into every stitch around the circle (see diagram).

This bracelet is both beautiful and simple to make. This is a good project for beginners because the beads are big, the thread is thick, and the hook size is large.

The pattern of alternating colors will help you see where your next stitch should go.

Blue beads are always bead crocheted into blue bead stitches and cream into cream.

Blue & White Stripe
by Mary Libby Neiman
MATERIALS:
9-10 yards Conso nylon thread • 16 grams size 6° Japanese seed beads (Blue, Cream) • 1.5 - 1.75 mm hook • #24 tapestry needle
STRING: Alternate 1 Blue, 1 Cream. • Repeat 71-80 times.
CONSTRUCTION:
Make 6 Bead-Chain stitches, leaving an 8" tail. Join beaded chain into a circle.

Make a Bead-Slip stitch in every stitch until tube measures 8"-9".
Slip stitch one more row with no beads.
Leave hook in the last loop, cut thread leaving a 12" tail. Put this cut end of tail through the last loop, remove crochet hook and tighten. • Thread 12" tail through a needle. Match a Blue bead on one end to a Blue bead on the other end and stitch through the 2 Blue beads to sew the ends of the bead tube together.

Stitch into a Cream bead, matching to a Cream bead on the other side. Continue two more times, matching Cream to Cream and Blue to Blue until the join is complete. Your join will be less visible if you stitch through the end bead and the one of the same color just behind it each time you make a stitch.

Beginner

Same Pattern - Different Size Beads

Size 11° Seed Beads create a thin tube.

Size 8° Seed Beads create a thicker tube.

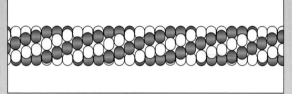

Size 6° Seed Beads create a thick tube.

Q What thread should I use?

A There are several good choices for thread that work well.

How tightly you work and how much wear a piece will receive will help determine thread choice for a bead crochet project.

Polyester threads like *YLI* Jean Stitch and *On the Surface* New Metallic are especially strong for their size (weight/thickness/fineness).

Conso 6 ply nylon is heavier and stronger and a fine choice to use with size 6° seed beads.

Gudebrod's E and F weight silk twist is strong and flexible.

Coats & Clark Extra strong thread for buttons and carpet is easily available.

Not as strong as nylon, polyester or silk are the good perle cotton threads from *DMC*. #5 and #8 perle cotton are very popular sizes for bead crochet and are easy to find.

DMC's Cebilia (tatting) thread is a smooth and somewhat stronger cotton choice.

This project is simple because triangle beads position nicely when crocheted 6 beads around. The triangle shapes fit together perfectly to form a neat circle with a mosaic-like surface.

Simple Tube Bracelet with Triangle Beads
by Mary Libby Neiman

MATERIALS:
7 1/2 yards thread • 7 grams size 11° triangle beads • Steel 1.15 - 1.25 mm hook • Needles (#24 tapestry and #10 beading) • Bracelet clasp • Hypo Cement

STRING: 1 yard of beads.

CONSTRUCTION:
Make 6 Bead-Chain stitches leaving a 12" tail. Join beaded chain into a circle.

Make a Bead-Slip stitch into every stitch until tube measures 8" or more as needed.

Leave hook in the last stitch. Cut thread leaving a 12" tail.

Thread tail through the last loop, remove crochet hook and tighten. Sew 1/2 of clasp on each end.

Bury threads in the body of the bead crochet tube and exit 1/2" from the join. Glue thread at exit. Let dry and trim.

Easy

hot red & blue

by Mary Libby Neiman

Wear this ruby red bracelet when you are feeling bold and sassy. It will brighten up any outfit, from jeans to that "little black dress".

Red Thick & Thin Bracelet

Tip: When this bracelet is bead crocheted with 5 repeats using Japanese seed beads, the tube should measure 8 1/2" before joining into a bracelet. If you need it to be much larger, add a 6th repeat. If you only need 1/2" or so longer, add 6 or 7 size 11° beads to each repeat. Adjust for other lengths by adding more size 8° or size 6° beads to each repeat. Also watch your tension as you change beads.

MATERIALS: 8 1/2 yards thread • Beads (100 size 6° seeds, 131 size 8° seeds, 265 size 11° seeds) • Steel 1.3 - 1.5 mm hook • Needle (#24 tapestry or #10 beading) • Hypo Cement
STRING: 53 size 11° seeds, 26 size 8° seeds, 20 size 6° seeds, 26 size 8° seeds. • Repeat 4 times for a total of 5 sets.
CONSTRUCTION: Make 6 Bead-Chain stitches. Join beaded chain into a circle. Make a Bead-Slip stitch into every stitch until tube measures 8 1/2" or more as needed. • Leave hook in the last loop to hold it open. Cut thread leaving a 12" tail. Pull cut end of the tail through the last loop, remove the crochet hook and tighten loop.
Thread one tail through a needle and sew the two ends together, needle weaving from one side to the other. Keep stitches tight to avoid gaps in the join. • Thread the other tail, repeat needle weaving for a few stitches. Bury threads in body of the bead crochet tube and exit 1/2" from the join. Glue thread at exit. Let dry and trim.

Jade cubes float above a sea of royal blue seed beads on this simple bracelet. Make it today. Wear it tonight.

Royal Blue & Jade Trim Bracelet

Tip: This pattern produces a straight row of cube beads. Be sure to keep this "straight row" pattern when fastening the clasp.

MATERIALS: 8 yards thread • Beads (306 Royal Blue size 8° seeds, 18 Jade Green 4 mm cubes) • Steel 1.4 - 1.6 mm hook • #24 tapestry needle • Bracelet clasp • Hypo Cement
STRING: 17 size 8°, 1 cube. • Repeat 17 times.
CONSTRUCTION: Make 4 Bead-Chain stitches, leaving an 8" tail. Join beaded chain into a circle. • Make a Bead-Slip stitch in every stitch until tube measures 8". Check for correct fit, allowing for the addition of a clasp. Add or subtract more beads and Bead Crochet stitches as needed. • Leave hook in last loop, cut thread leaving a 12" tail. Pull cut end of tail through the last loop, remove crochet hook and tighten.
Insert 1 thread through a needle and sew one side of clasp to one end of crocheted tube. • Repeat with other side of clasp, attaching it to the other end of the tube. • Bury threads in the body of the bead crochet tube and exit 1/2" from the join. Glue thread at exit. Let dry and trim.

Two different sizes of beads give texture to these projects. Feel the warmth of amber colors with the Golden Earth stripe bracelet or create a bolder look with the Magenta and Silver stripe.

Golden Earth Stripe

4 around, 2 bead sizes

MATERIALS:
8 yards thread • Japanese seed beads (9 grams size 6° Matte Topaz Rainbow, 6 grams size 8° Topaz Rainbow) • 1.4 - 1.75 mm hook • Needle (#24 tapestry or #10 beading)
STRING: 2 Matte Topaz, 2 Topaz. • Repeat 62-74 times.
CONSTRUCTION:
Make 4 Bead-Chain stitches, leaving an 8" tail. Join beaded chain into a circle. • Make a Bead-Slip stitch in every stitch until tube measures 8"-9". • Slip stitch one more row with no beads. Leave hook in the last loop, cut thread leaving a 12" tail. Put this cut end of tail through the last loop, remove crochet hook and tighten.

Thread 12" tail through a needle. Match 2 Matte Topaz beads on one end to the 2 Matte Topaz beads on the other end and begin stitching the two ends together.

Match the 2 Topaz beads on each end and continue stitching until join is complete.

> " Make it elegant, or make it fun, but definitely make it yourself "
>
> – Mary Libby Neiman

Magenta and Silver Stripe

6 around, 2 bead sizes

MATERIALS: 8-9 yards thread • Japanese seed beads (15 grams size 6° Magenta, 9 grams size 8° Silvery Crystal) • 1.4 - 1.75 mm hook • Needle (#24 tapestry or #10 beading)
STRING:
3 Magenta, 3 Silvery Crystal. • Repeat 66-76 times.
CONSTRUCTION:
Make 6 Bead-Chain stitches, leaving an 8" tail. Join beaded chain into a circle. Make a Bead-Slip stitch in every stitch until tube measures 8"-9". • Slip stitch one more row with no beads. Leave hook in the last loop, cut thread leaving a 12" tail. Put this cut end of tail through the last loop, remove crochet hook and tighten.

Thread 12" tail through a needle. Match the 3 Magenta beads on one end to the 3 Magenta beads on the other end, begin stitching the two ends together. Matching the 3 Silvery Crystal beads on each end, continue stitching until the join is complete. • Test your join by pulling gently on each side of it. If you see a noticeable amount of thread, undo your stitching and re-stitch with tighter stitches.

baubles
bangles
& beads

by Mary Libby Neiman

Gold, copper, silver and black metallics are so elegant. They are perfect for that Black-Tie New Year's Eve event. These bracelets will also dress up an everyday outfit. Wear a copper or silver bracelet with boots and jeans. Refine business casual wear with gorgeous gold or understated black. This is the perfect project for beginners because you get such stunning results, no one will believe you made it yourself.

One simple stitch, repeated many times, provides the practice you need to perfect your skill. Make several bracelets and you will have your Christmas list completed in no time. As your confidence and skill increase, you'll want to make the matching necklaces.

Simple Tube Bangles

MATERIALS:
8 yards thread • 8-9 grams size 8 hex beads • Steel 1.3 - 1.5 mm hook • Needles (#24 tapestry and #10 beading) • Hypo Cement
STRING:
Approximately 1 yard beads.
CONSTRUCTION:
Make 4 Bead-Chain stitches, leaving an 8" tail. Join beaded chain into a circle. • Make a Bead-Slip stitch in every stitch until the tube measures 8"-9".

Leave hook in last loop to hold it open. Cut thread leaving a 12" tail. Pull cut end of tail through the last loop, remove crochet hook and tighten loop.

Thread 1 end through a needle and sew the 2 ends of the tube together, needle weaving from one side to the other. Keep stitches tight to avoid gaps in the join.

Thread other end and repeat needle weaving for a few stitches. Bury threads in the body of the bead crochet tube and exit 1/2" from the join. Glue thread at exit. Let dry and trim.

opposites attract

Easy

by Mary Libby Neiman

These classy black and gold chains look great separately or together, and they are so easy to make you will have them ready in a flash!

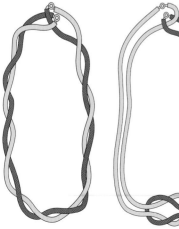
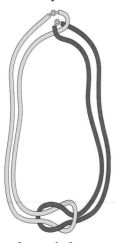

| Twist 2 neck-laces together | Loop-de-Loop Knot, see page 11 | Simple Overhand Knot |

Easy

Both necklaces are crocheted exactly the same, the difference is that the bead colors are switched.

Black & Gold Double Necklace

MATERIALS: Beads size 8 hex cut (864 Black, 150 Gold) • 28-30 yards thread • Steel 1.3 - 1.5 mm hook • Needles (#24 tapestry and #10 beading) • Necklace clasp • Hypo Cement

STRING: 6 Black, 1 Gold.

Repeat 143 times. Strung beads will measure 10'. • You may find it easier to string 72 repeats and Bead Crochet 14" of the tube. Leave 7 beads to remind you of the pattern. • Unwind the thread and rethread needle. • When you begin to string the beads again, check to be sure you are continuing in the same pattern.

**Since the last bead of the seven you left unworked will be <u>Black,</u> you must reverse the stringing pattern and start with <u>1 Gold, then 6 Black.</u> • Repeat 71 times.

CONSTRUCTION:

Make 4 Bead-Chain stitches, leaving an 8" tail. Join beaded chain into a circle. Make a Bead-Slip stitch in every stitch until tube measures 28".

Leave hook in last loop to hold it open. Cut thread leaving a 12" tail. Pull cut end of tail through the last loop, remove crochet hook and tighten loop.

Insert one thread through a tapestry needle and sew one side of clasp to one end of crocheted tube.

Repeat with other side of clasp, attaching it to the other end of the tube.

Bury threads in the body of the bead crochet tube and exit 1/2" from the join. Glue thread at exit. Let dry and trim.

Gold & Black Double Necklace

MATERIALS: Beads size 8 hex cut (864 Gold, 150 Black)

STRING: 6 Gold, 1 Black.

**Since the last bead of the seven you left unworked will be <u>Gold</u>, you must reverse the stringing pattern and start with <u>1 Black, then 6 Gold.</u>

How to Make a Loop-de-Loop Knot

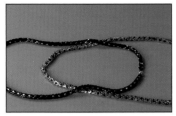

1. Lay the Black necklace over Gold necklace.

2. Lift inside loops.

3. Pass the Gold loop over Black loop. Pull gently to form the knot.

4. Adjust the knot so each clasp is at the back of the necklace.

" ... join the hottest craft revival to come along in a good while! "

– Suzanne McNeill

sporty spice

by Mary Libby Neiman

This easy-to-make bracelet has one nice advantage - the closure allows you to change large hole beads for different looks. Add a magnetic clasp for easy "off and on."

Beginner

Raspberry Bracelet with Magnetic Clasp

MATERIALS: 9 yards thread • Beads (14 grams 8° Delica or 'Treasure' beads), 1 large hole silver bead, to cover the magnetic clasp • 1 small magnetic clasp • Steel 1.4 - 1.6 mm hook • Needles #24 tapestry and #10 beading) • Hypo Cement
STRING: 14 grams of beads.
CONSTRUCTION:
Make 5 Bead-Chain stitches leaving an 18" tail. Join beaded chain into a circle.

Make a Bead-Slip stitch in every stitch until tube measures 7 1/2". • Leave hook in the last loop, cut thread leaving an 18" tail. Pull cut end of tail through the last loop, remove crochet hook and tighten.

Add the magnetic clasp. Thread needle and stitch 2 times through the last row of Bead-Slip stitches. Make 3 Chain stitches. Put needle through the last Chain stitch. Put needle through the shank (loop) of one half of the magnetic clasp. • Stitch into the last Chain stitch again, then through the clasp again. Repeat for added strength. • Weave threaded needle through the Chain stitches and then insert into the body of the tube. Stitch back and forth through the tube twice, glue thread, let dry and trim. • Repeat for the other side of the tube and the other half of the clasp.

Before finishing the chain on this side, check to see that there are no gaps when the two sides of the magnetic clasp meet inside the large hole bead. If they do not meet, add a Chain stitch or two. If there is a gap between the body of the tube and the ends of the large hole bead when the clasp is connected inside the large hole bead, remove a Chain stitch or two.

> **"As artists combine new fiber techniques with old crochet patterns, bead crochet is being reinvented."**
>
> – Mary Libby Neiman

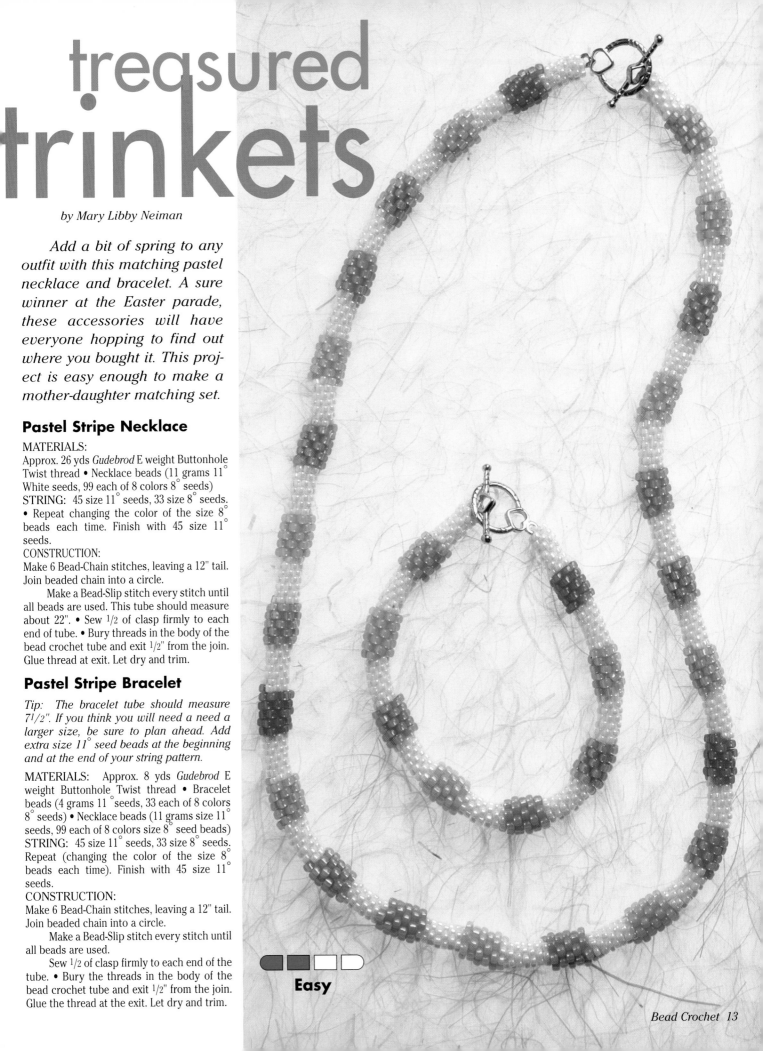

treasured trinkets

by Mary Libby Neiman

Add a bit of spring to any outfit with this matching pastel necklace and bracelet. A sure winner at the Easter parade, these accessories will have everyone hopping to find out where you bought it. This project is easy enough to make a mother-daughter matching set.

Pastel Stripe Necklace

MATERIALS:
Approx. 26 yds *Gudebrod* E weight Buttonhole Twist thread • Necklace beads (11 grams 11° White seeds, 99 each of 8 colors 8° seeds)
STRING: 45 size 11° seeds, 33 size 8° seeds. • Repeat changing the color of the size 8° beads each time. Finish with 45 size 11° seeds.
CONSTRUCTION:
Make 6 Bead-Chain stitches, leaving a 12" tail. Join beaded chain into a circle.

Make a Bead-Slip stitch every stitch until all beads are used. This tube should measure about 22". • Sew 1/2 of clasp firmly to each end of tube. • Bury threads in the body of the bead crochet tube and exit 1/2" from the join. Glue thread at exit. Let dry and trim.

Pastel Stripe Bracelet

Tip: The bracelet tube should measure 7 1/2". If you think you will need a need a larger size, be sure to plan ahead. Add extra size 11° seed beads at the beginning and at the end of your string pattern.

MATERIALS: Approx. 8 yds *Gudebrod* E weight Buttonhole Twist thread • Bracelet beads (4 grams 11° seeds, 33 each of 8 colors 8° seeds) • Necklace beads (11 grams size 11° seeds, 99 each of 8 colors size 8° seed beads)
STRING: 45 size 11° seeds, 33 size 8° seeds. Repeat (changing the color of the size 8° beads each time). Finish with 45 size 11° seeds.
CONSTRUCTION:
Make 6 Bead-Chain stitches, leaving a 12" tail. Join beaded chain into a circle.

Make a Bead-Slip stitch every stitch until all beads are used.

Sew 1/2 of clasp firmly to each end of the tube. • Bury the threads in the body of the bead crochet tube and exit 1/2" from the join. Glue the thread at the exit. Let dry and trim.

Easy

Easy

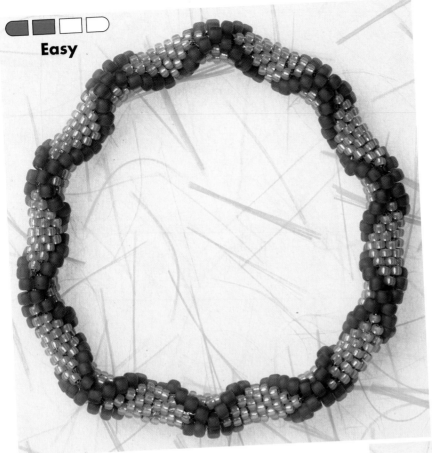

Criss Cross Bangles

MATERIALS:

8 yards thread • Beads (231 dark color size 8° seeds, 525 light color size 11° seeds) • Steel 1.25 - 1.4 mm hook • #10 beading needle • Hypo Cement

STRING: 1 size 8° • 2 size 11° • 1 size 8° • 3 size 11° • 1 size 8° • 1 size 11° • 1 size 8° • 4 size 11° • 2 size 8° • 5 size 11° • 2 size 8° • 4 size 11° • 1 size 8° • 1 size 11° • 1 size 8° • 3 size 11° • 1 size 8° • 2 size 11°. • Repeat pattern 20 times.

CONSTRUCTION:

Make 6 Bead-Chain stitches leaving a 12" tail. Join beaded chain into a circle.

Make a Bead-Slip stitch in every stitch until tube measures $8^{1}/2$" - 9".

Before joining ends, check to see that the joined bracelet will slide over your hand. Add one or more complete repeats if necessary.

Leave hook in last loop to hold it open. Cut thread leaving a 12" tail. Pull cut end of tail through the last loop, remove crochet hook and tighten loop. • Sew ends together by needle weaving. Be sure to match the pattern carefully before joining. Keep stitches tight to avoid gaps in the join.

Bury threads in the body of the bead crochet tube and exit $1/2$" from the join. Glue thread at exit. Let dry and trim.

into the groove

by Mary Libby Neiman

These bracelets get their intricate design from the way the beads are strung. You will have a much easier time making this bracelet if you make a stringing sample and tape it to your workspace. Once the beads are ready, simply crochet the same stitch over and over. The bracelet pattern will appear like magic.

signature piece

by Mary Libby Neiman

A very simple stringing pattern makes a beautiful effect in this pin that can also be worn as a necklace pendant. Change the gold to silver to match southwest style apparel. Use the left-over beads to make matching earrings for a complete ensemble.

Turquoise & Gold Circle Pin or Pendant

MATERIALS: $8^{1}/2$ yards thread • Size $11^{°}$ seed beads (750 Turquoise, 150 Gold) • Steel 1.25 - 1.4 mm hook • #10 beading needle • Hypo Cement • Bar pin back

STRING: 5 Turquoise, 1 Gold. • Repeat until 42" are strung.

CONSTRUCTION:

Make 6 Bead-Chain stitches, leaving an 8" tail. • Join beaded chain into a circle.

Make a Bead-Slip stitch in every stitch until tube measures $8^{1}/2$". • Leave hook in last loop to hold it open. Cut thread leaving a 12" tail. Pull cut end of tail through the last loop, remove crochet hook and tighten loop. • Tie tube in a loose knot. Wind each end around loop until knot resembles the illustration.

Check to see that there are 5 ridges on the outer edge. • Join ends, matching Gold bead on one end to the Gold bead on the other end. Thread 1 tail through a needle and sew ends together carefully.

Thread second tail. Sew 2-3 stitches back and forth to reinforce join. • Bury threads in the body of the bead crochet tube and exit $1/2$" from the join. Glue thread at exit. Let dry and trim.

Stitch a small pin back (with loops to allow wearing as a pendant) on the back of the twisted circle. Position carefully so pin back does not show from the front.

Tying the Tube

Tie tube in a loose knot. Wind each end around loop until the knot resembles the illustration.

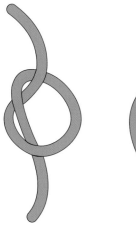
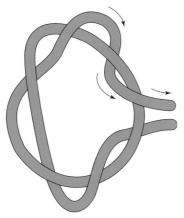

Easy

go for

by Mary Libby Neiman

These bracelets are fascinating because the spiral appears to have no beginning or end. They get their depth and texture from 3 different sizes of beads.

Red, Yellow & Turquoise Zig Zag Bracelet

MATERIALS: 9 yards *On the Surface* New Metallic thread • Beads (116 size 6° Matte Turquoise, 232 size 8° Yellow seeds, 348 size 11° Matte Red seeds) • Steel 1.25 - 1.4 mm hook • Needles (#24 tapestry and #10 beading) • Hypo Cement

STRING: 3 size 11° • 1 size 8° • 1 size 6° • 1 size 8°. • Repeat 115 times.

CONSTRUCTION:

Make 6 Bead-Chain stitches, leaving a 12" tail. Join beaded chain into a circle. • Continue with a Bead-Slip stitch in the next stitch and every stitch until the tube measures 8$^{1}/_{2}$".

Check for correct size. To make a larger or smaller size, add or subtract as many beads and bead crochet repeats as necessary. • Cut thread, leaving a 12" tail. Pull cut end of tail through the last loop, remove crochet hook and tighten loop. Thread tail through needle. • Match Turquoise bead on one end to the Turquoise bead on the other end. Stitch back and forth. Continue stitching, matching beads on one end to beads on the other end. Keep stitches tight to avoid gaps in the join. • Thread 12" tail and stitch into and out of the tube twice. • Bury threads in the body of the bead crochet tube and exit $^{1}/_{2}$" from the join. Glue thread at exit. Let dry and trim.

Intermediate

Pink, Opal & Matte Gold - Zig Zag Bracelets

Tip: This tube will be a little tricky to keep firmly crocheted because there is a dramatic difference in the size of the beads. Be sure to tighten your thread carefully after each stitch. Check occasionally to see that the tube is spiraling evenly.

MATERIALS: 9 yards *On the Surface* New Metallic thread • Beads (116 faceted 4mm Pink Crystal, 232 size 8° Matte Gold seeds, 348 size 11° Opal seeds) • Steel 1.25 - 1.4 mm hook • Needles (#24 tapestry and #10 beading) • Hypo Cement

STRING: 3 size 11° • 1 size 8° • 1 crystal • 1 size 8°. • Repeat 115 times.

CONSTRUCTION:

Make 6 Bead-Chain stitches, leaving a 12" tail. Join beaded chain into a circle. • Continue with a Bead-Slip stitch in the next stitch and every stitch until the tube measures 8$^{1}/_{2}$". • Check for correct size. To make a larger or smaller size, add or subtract as many beads and bead crochet repeats as necessary. • Cut thread, leaving a 12" tail. Pull cut end of tail through the last loop, remove crochet hook and tighten loop. Thread tail through needle.

Match crystal bead on one end to the crystal bead on the other end. Stitch back and forth. • Continue stitching, matching beads on one end to beads on the other end. Keep stitches tight to avoid gaps in the join.

Thread 12" tail and stitch into and out of the tube twice.

Bury threads in the body of the bead crochet tube and exit $^{1}/_{2}$" from the join. Glue thread at exit. Let dry and trim.

Surround your crocheted flower center with beautiful silk ribbon petals for an eye-catching accessory.

Ribbon Flower
by Janie Ray

MATERIALS: Wire edged ribbon (1 1/2" wide 14" long, 3/4" wide 11" long) • Needle • Thread • Bar pin back

INSTRUCTIONS:

Gather both pieces of ribbon by pulling the wire on one side.

Gather with a needle and thread into tight circles.

Sew smaller circle onto larger one. • Sew crochet flower in center. Add pin to the back.

ABBREVIATIONS:
ch = Chain
YO = yarn over
st = stitch
beg = beginning
sl st = Slip stitch
sc = Single Crochet
dc = Double Crochet
(B) = reminder that this row uses beads
b in front of stitch name = beads are included in that stitch
blp = Bead Loop. When more than one bead is included before doing a YO, a number will indicate how many beads should be pulled up to form the loop.

www.learntocrochet.com

Beaded Looped Flower
by Janet Ohle

MATERIALS: 4 yards *Gudebrod Inc* Violet #5263 size F Champion Silk Thread • 360 seed beads • Steel 1.4 mm hook • Beading needle

STRING:
Beads on silk thread. Leave an 8" tail for finishing.

CONSTRUCTION:
Work over tail or weave in as desired.

Rnd 1: Ch 2

Rnd 2: 6 sc in second ch from hook

Rnd 3: 2 sc in each sc around (12)

Rnd 4: Pull up 30 beads and bsc in first sc. Repeat, making a bead loop of 30 beads in each sc (12 loops made). Sl st in first sc, fasten off and weave in ends.

Rnd 5: Join thread with a sc to the center of one bead loop (15 beads on each side of newly joined thread), ch 1, sc in center of next loop, ch 1. Continue working sc, ch 1 in each bead loop around. Join with a sl st in first sc.

Rnd 6: Draw up a loop in the space in between every other sc around (under ch 1), pull loop through all loops to bring loops together and ch 2.

Leaving an 8" tail, fasten off.

Thread both tails through the opposite side of initial ch in Rnd. 1. Pull tightly, knot securely and weave in ends.

How to Make a Ribbon Flower

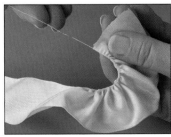

1. Pull the wire out of one edge of the ribbon to begin gathering.

2. Use a Running stitch and strong thread to gather one edge tightly.

3. Sew the smaller ribbon circle onto the larger one.

4. Sew the beaded flower in the center.

Polymer Clay beads by Karen Lewis, contact her at www.klewexpressions.com

Mermaid glass bead by Mavis Smith, contact her at www.mavissmith.com

Spiky Necklace

MATERIALS:
Beads (Pink size 8° seeds, Cobalt Iris size 8° seeds, Teal Iris size 8° seeds) • 1 tube Gutermann Aqua daggers • Needle (#24 tapestry or #10 beading) • Hypo Cement

FOCAL BEAD:
Large beautiful bead • 2 Silver 5 mm spacer beads • 2 Silver end-caps • 2 Silver 5 mm split rings • 1 toggle and bolt clasp set • 20 gauge beading wire 8" long

DAGGER BEAD SECTIONS:
Conso #69 upholstery thread • Steel 1.15 - 1.2 mm hook

STRING:
10" of dagger beads

CONSTRUCTION:
Make 5 Bead-Chain stitches, leaving a 12" tail. Join beaded chain into a circle. • Continue with a Bead-Slip stitch in the next stitch and every stitch until all the beads are used.

Cut thread, leaving a 12" tail. Pull cut end of tail through the last loop, remove crochet hook and tighten loop.

Repeat with a new thread for the second section.

SEED BEAD SECTIONS:
Conso #18 upholstery thread • Steel 1.5 mm hook

STRING: 2 pink, 4 other (Cobalt and Teal mix). • Repeat until about 25" of thread is filled.

CONSTRUCTION:
Make 5 Bead-Chain stitches, leaving a 12" tail. Join beaded chain into a circle. • Continue with a Bead-Slip stitch in the next stitch and every stitch until all beads used.

Cut thread, leaving a 12" tail. Pull cut end of tail through the last loop, remove crochet hook and tighten loop. Thread 12" tail onto needle. Add cap bead and 1 end of the necklace clasp. Sew down into crochet tube several times. Come back through the clasp again. Sew down into crochet tube again. Bring thread out. Knot, glue, and trim end.

Repeat stringing and construction for second section.

FOCAL BEAD:
Thread wire through bead. Thread small Silver bead onto wire. Make a loop in the end. Wrap the tail of the wire around the base of the loop. • Repeat for other end.

NECKLACE CONSTRUCTION:
Using 12" tails from Seed Bead section and Dagger section, needle weave the pieces together.

Repeat with other Seed Bead and Dagger section. Keep stitches tight to avoid gaps in the join.

Thread remaining tail of one Dagger section. Sew to wire loop at one end of the focal bead. Sew into the Dagger tube and back through wire loop again. Sew down into Dagger tube again. Bring thread out. Knot, glue, and trim end.

Repeat for other end of focal bead.

Attaching the Focal Bead

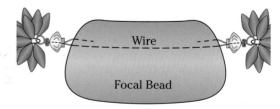

Pass 20 gauge wire through the focal bead. Add a small bead to wire. Make a loop, twist wire and pass it back through the small bead.

Twist it again, then bind the end in the focal bead. Repeat at the other end of the focal bead.

Attach necklace to the wire loop on each side of the bead.

the changelings

The beads in this ensemble really bring out the colors in the glass focal bead. The swirling pattern in the necklace is achieved by a simple stringing order.

Experienced

Great color choice makes this bracelet pleasing to the eye. Choose beads that complement each other for your own unique effect. Make your own line of accessories to match your wardrobe.

the changelings

Add a focal bead to your bracelet and change the whole look!

Polymer Clay beads by Karen Lewis, contact her at www.klewexpressions.com

Basic Spiky Bracelet, pictured above

MATERIALS: Beads (Pink size $8°$ seeds, Cobalt Iris size $8°$ seeds, Teal Iris size $8°$ seeds) • Gutermann Aqua daggers • Needle (#24 tapestry or #10 beading) • Hypo Cement

<u>DAGGER BEAD SECTION:</u>
Conso #69 upholstery thread, Steel 1.15 - 1.2 mm hook
STRING 5" of dagger beads.
CONSTRUCTION:
Make 5 Bead-Chain stitches, leaving a 12" tail. Join beaded chain into a circle. • Continue with a Bead-Slip stitch in the next stitch and every stitch until all the beads are used. • Cut thread, leaving a 12" tail. Pull cut end of tail through the last loop, remove crochet hook and tighten loop.

<u>SEED BEAD SECTIONS:</u>
Conso #18 upholstery thread, Steel 1.5 mm hook
STRING: 2 pink, 4 other (Iris & Teal mix). • Repeat until about 34" of thread is filled.
CONSTRUCTION: Make 5 Bead-Chain stitches, leaving a 12" tail. Join beaded chain into a circle. • Continue with a Bead-Slip stitch in the next stitch and every stitch until all beads used.
    Cut thread, leaving a 12" tail. Pull cut end of tail through the last loop, remove crochet hook and tighten loop. Thread 12" tail onto needle.

BRACELET CONSTRUCTION:
Using 12" tails from Seed Bead section and Dagger Bead section, needle weave the pieces together. Sew down into crochet tube several times. Bring thread out. Knot, glue and trim end. • Repeat for second section.
OPTIONAL: Add a focal bead (see page 18).

lime green & shine

by Mary Libby Neiman

Glass leaves glitter like crystals in the light when you wear this attractive necklace. Make it in your favorite pastel color. The glass leaves will complement any choice, and you will receive compliments every time you wear this pretty accessory.

Lime Green & Crystal Drop Leaf Necklace

Tip: The leaf is strung so that it does not spiral around like the seed beads. It appears next to the previous leaf when the necklace is flat. You must take care, when you put the necklace on, that you maintain this linear effect. Because the crocheted tube is so flexible, it is quite easy to accidentally twist it and the leaves. Check in a mirror before fastening the clasp.

MATERIALS:
21 yards thread • Beads (30 grams size 8° seeds, 42 glass leaves or drop beads) • Steel 1.4 - 1.5 mm hook • Needles (#24 tapestry and #10 beading) • Necklace clasp • Hypo Cement
STRING:
22 seeds, 1 leaf. • Repeat 41 times.
CONSTRUCTION:
Make 4 Bead-Chain stitches, leaving an 8" tail. Join beaded chain into a circle.

Make a Bead-Slip stitch in every stitch until tube measures 22". • Leave hook in last loop, cut thread leaving a 12" tail. Pull cut end of tail through the last loop, remove crochet hook and tighten. • Insert one thread through a needle and sew one side of clasp to one end of the crocheted tube.

Repeat with other side of the clasp, attaching it to the other end of the tube.

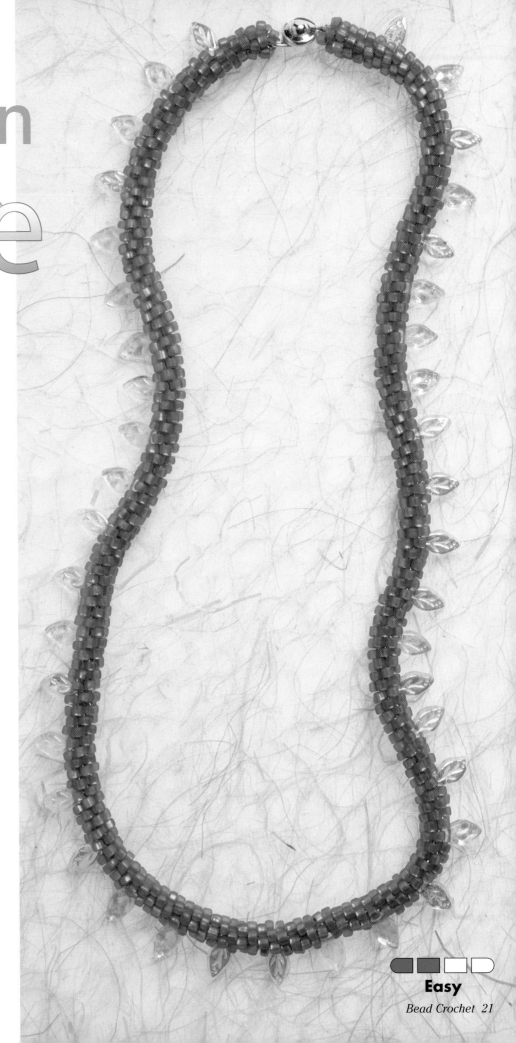

Easy

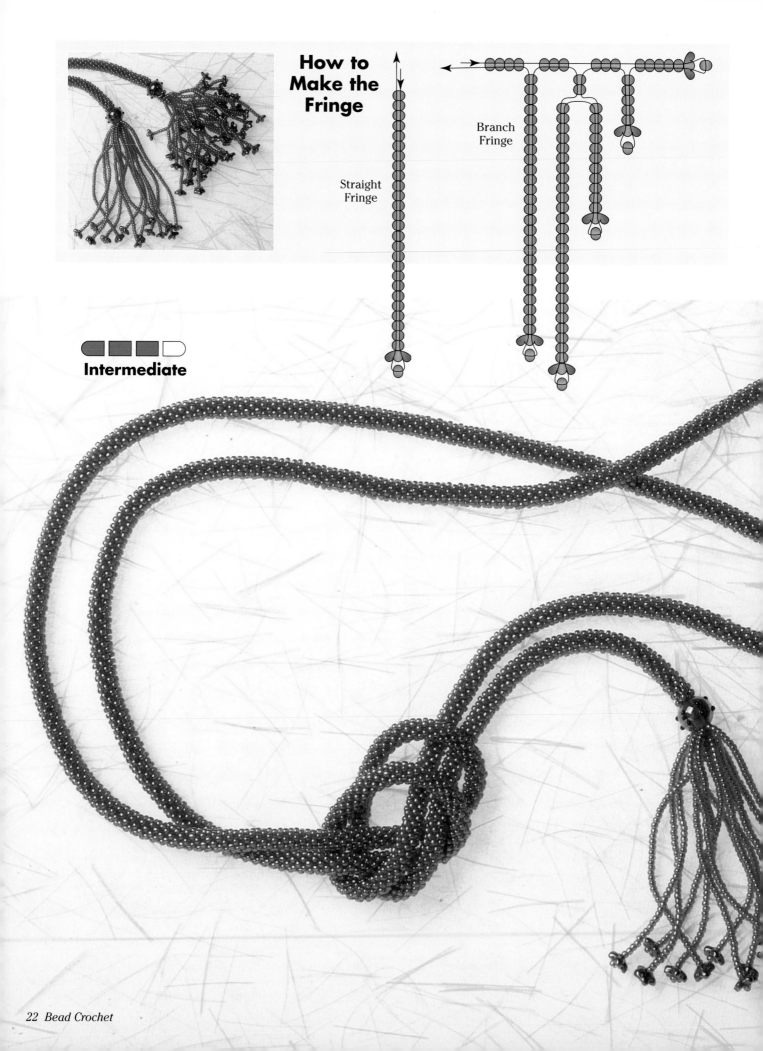

How to Make the Fringe

Straight Fringe

Branch Fringe

Intermediate

Dripping with fringe, lariat style necklaces were very popular in the Roaring 20's. Update this nostalgic look with your 21st century rendition of a classic wearable art.

the golden topaz look

by Mary Libby Neiman

Gold Luster Topaz Fringed Lariat

handmade lampwork beads by Larry Scott. contact him at www.larryscott.net

MATERIALS: 75 yards thread • Beads (70 grams size 11° seeds, 60 glass flower shape, 2 lampwork 14 mm with large hole) • Steel 1.15 – 1.3 mm hook • Needles (#24 tapestry, #10 beading and #12 twisted wire) • Hypo Cement

STRING: 2 yards of seed beads. Leave 6" tails and bury the tails into the tube later, gluing lightly where they exit after a few stitches and trimming them nicely so that no extra thread is visible. • Continue to string beads on thread and add to previous work until desired length is reached. • Lariat shown is 58" before fringe.

CONSTRUCTION:

Make 5 Bead-Chain stitches, leaving an 8" tail. Join bead chain into a circle. •

Make a Bead-Slip stitch in every stitch until it is time to add more strung beads and thread. Join threads and continue until desired length is reached.

Leave hook in last loop to hold it open. Cut thread leaving a 30" tail. Pull cut end of tail through the last loop, remove crochet hook and tighten loop.

STRAIGHT FRINGE:

Cut 3 threads 34" long. Use a needle to run each thread through the body of the loop, 1/2" from the end. Thread each end back into the body of the tube, one bead away from where the thread exited. Point the needle down the center of the tube and push the needle until it exits at the center bottom of the tube. • Repeat until all 7 threads are hanging from the bottom of the tube. • Bring all 7 ends through the hole in 1 lampwork bead. For ease in handling, you may want to temporarily tape the lampwork bead to the body of the tube so it does not slip down the threads as the fringe is worked. Once several fringe pieces have been completed with beads, they will hold the large bead in place. • Use a beading needle to string 45 size 11° seed beads on one thread, add 1 flower bead, add 1 size 11°. • Insert needle back into the flower bead, tightening the thread, and back through the 45 size 11° seed beads. Keep the thread taut, tightening it up as the thread returns through the seed beads. Make sure the beads all touch one another with no thread showing between them. • Repeat with the other 6 threads. • Keep checking the lengths of fringe against the other lengths. Seed beads vary in size and you may need to make adjustments in the number of beads to keep each fringe element close in length to the finished fringe. • After all 7 threads are strung and returned to the bottom of the tube, tie each one to at least one other thread with a firm square knot. Continue threading 45 seed beads, 1 flower shape and 1 seed bead and passing the needle and thread back through the flower and 45 seed beads to the base of the tube. Do this with each of the 7 threads. • Once all 7 threads are returned, through beads, to the base of the tube, tie them once again into firm square knots to at least one other thread. All 7 threads are now passed up through the lampwork bead and tied once more. Glue knots. Let dry and trim.

BRANCH FRINGE:

Cut 4-5 threads 34" long. This thread is added to the body of the tube in the same way, all passing out through the bottom of the tube. • String 40-45 size 11° seed beads, add 1 flower, add 1 size 11° seed bead. Pass thread back through the flower bead and some of the size 11° seed beads. • To make the fringe branch, stop at a point before returning through all the seed beads and exit out of the fringe. Add several size 11° seed beads (vary the amount from 10-25), add 1 flower and 1 size 11° seed bead. • Return through the flower bead and exit before returning to the base of the tube. Do this 2-4 times for each main fringe thread. Finish by tying, gluing and trimming ends.

fine arts

The different ends on this lariat make it interesting. This easy necklace is the result of many repeated slip stitches.

Turquoise Lariat with Bead and Tassel

by Mary Libby Neiman
handmade lampwork bead by Robert Jennik
contact him at 414-771-8360

MATERIALS: 60 yards thread • Beads (80 grams size 8° seeds, 1 Silver tassel, 1 Lampwork) • Steel 1.4 - 1.6 mm hook • #24 tapestry needle • Hypo Cement

STRING: 2 yards of size 8° seeds. • You will add more beads after these beads have been crocheted.

CONSTRUCTION:
Make 4 Bead-Chain stitches, leaving an 18" tail. Join beaded chain into a circle.

Make a Bead-Slip stitch in every stitch until the 2 yards of beads have been crocheted. • Cut the thread, leaving an 8" tail. String 2 more yards of size 8° beads. Tie the two threads in a square knot close to the center of the tube, leaving 6" tails to be stitched in, glued and trimmed later. • Continue Bead-Slip stitch crochet, adding beads as needed. Lariat shown is 60". When tube has reached desired length, stop. Leave hook in the last loop and cut thread leaving a 24" tail. Pull cut end of tail through the last loop, remove hook and tighten loop. • Thread 18" tail through needle and sew Silver tassel firmly to one end of the tube. Bury excess thread in the body of the tube after stitching in and out of the tube twice. Glue, let dry and trim thread. • Thread the needle with the tail on the other end of the tube, pass needle through hole of the lampwork bead and then through 1 matching size 8° seed bead. Pass needle through the lampwork bead again, and into the body of the tube. Stitch through the tube twice and return needle back through the lampwork bead, seed bead and then the lampwork bead again, continuing into the body of the tube.

Stitch into the tube two more times. Glue and trim thread.

Easy

hit list

Surround your delicate beaded crochet flower with gorgeous silk ribbon petals. A silk stem and green leaves give a finishing touch to a creation as beautiful as the real thing.

Beaded Petal Flower
by Janet Ohle

MATERIALS: *Gudebrod Inc* Champion Silk Thread (2 yds Purple #5264 size F; 4 yds. Violet # 5263 Violet Size F) • *On the Surface* New Metallics Thread (3 yds. Alexandrite #16) • 70 Lavender or Violet size 11° seed beads • Steel 1.4 mm hook • Beading needle

CONSTRUCTION:
With Purple thread, Chain 2.

Rnd 1: 6 sc in second chain from hook (6 sc).

Rnd 2: 2 sc in back loop of each sc around (12 sc).

Rnd 3: Continue working in back loops as follows: 2 sc in first sc, 1 sc in next sc. • Repeat 5 times. (18 sc). • Finish off Purple thread and weave in end.

Rnd 4: Working in both loops, join Violet thread in any sc. Sc in same sc. • Chain 3, skip 2, sc in next sc. • Repeat until 6 loops are complete. Join with a Sl st in first sc.

Rnd 5: Sc in first chain space, ch 4, 5 triple popcorn in same chain loop, ch 4, sc in same loop, sc in next loop. • Repeat until 6 petals are complete. Sl st in first sc. Fasten off and weave in end.

Rnd 6: Transfer the seed beads to the metallic thread. • With wrong side facing you, attach metallic thread to any sc. Leave a 6" tail. • 3 bsc in next loop, 2 bsc in chain at top of petal, 3 bsc in next ch 4 loop, sc in next sc. • Repeat for each petal. Fasten off.

Rnd 7: Attach metallic thread to first free loop of Rnd 2. Work surface crochet bsc in same stitch and continue to work one surface bsc in free loops of Rnd 2. (12 surface bead sc's) Fasten off and weave in thread.

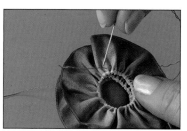

Intermediate

Making a Ribbon Flower and Leaves

1. Pull the wire out of one edge of the ribbon to begin gathering.

2. Use a Running stitch and strong thread to gather edge tightly.

3. Sew the layers of ribbon together.

4. Fold green ribbon in a triangle to make a leaf shape.

5. Fold ribbon again. Sew across the bottom to secure.

6. Sew leaves to a stem made of ribbon-wrapped wire.

7. Sew flower to stem.

Silk Ribbon Flower & Leaves
by Janie Ray

MATERIALS: Wire edged ribbon (5/8" wide variegated Purple 18" long, 3 pieces of 1 1/2" wide Green 3 1/2" long, 1 piece of 1 1/2" wide Green 10" long) • Stem wire 5" long • Needle • Thread • Bar pin back

INSTRUCTIONS:
Working from each end toward the center, remove wire then gather one edge of Purple ribbon. • Form half of ribbon into a small circle. Form remainder of ribbon into a slightly larger circle. Sew to secure. • Sew crocheted flower to center.
  Wrap wire with Green ribbon and sew ends to secure.
  Make 3 leaves.
  Sew leaves, flower, and pin back to end of stem. Curl the bottom of the stem.

glamour show off

by Janet Ohle

Beaded loops make a delicate texture on this copper and pink necklace. Choose your accent bead, then plan your project with coordinating bead colors. This is a great way to showcase that one-of-a-kind treasure in your bead box.

Beaded Loops Necklace

Tip: Tighten the thread after every loop to keep chains as tight as possible. If you would like a smaller diameter bead as an accent bead, you may need to begin with fewer chains.

Size: Approximately 24" length
MATERIALS: *On the Surface* New Metallics Thread • 1 hank size 11° seed beads • 1 large dichroic glass accent bead • Steel 1.4 mm hook • Beading needle
STRING:
Transfer the seed beads to the metallic thread. Leave a 6" tail.
CONSTRUCTION:
  Chain 8. • Pull up 5 beads for each loop. Chain past the fifth bead. This makes your first loop.
  Repeat 8 times. You now have 9 Chain stitches with 5 bead loops in each stitch.
  Pull up 6 beads and Chain past the sixth bead. • Repeat 14 times (15 Chain stitches with 6 bead loops in each stitch.)
  Pull up 7 beads and Chain. • Repeat until the necklace measures approximately 22".
  Pull up 6 beads and Chain past the sixth bead. • Repeat 14 times. • Pull up 5 beads and Chain past the fifth bead. • Repeat 8 times. Chain 8 and fasten off leaving a 6" tail.
FINISHING:
  Thread one of the tails with beading needle and take thread through your large bead. Thread the other tail through the needle and take it through the large bead in the opposite direction of the first tail. Stitch each end through the 8 Chain stitches of the opposite being careful not to split the thread. Then pull both tails tightly to bring the 8 Chains into the center of the large bead. Then sew through 2 or 3 of the Chains in the necklace, secure and fasten off. Cut thread close to your work.

5 bead loops

6 bead loops

> **In no time you will be proudly showing off your latest creation and planning your next.**
> – Suzanne McNeill

Easy

the amulet mystique

by Laurel Kubby

Crochet Amulet Bag

MATERIALS: *DMC* perle size #8 cotton (main thread) • 2 ply metallic thread (secondary thread) • Beads (45 grams size 11° mixed color seed beads that coordinate with the main thread color, 20 crystals or semi-precious beads 4-6 mm for the necklace strands, 1$^{1}/_{2}$" - 2" donut shaped pi stone to coordinate with the main thread) • Steel 1.6 - 1.8 mm hook • Beading supplies (size 10 needle, size D Nymo thread)

ABBREVIATIONS:
ch = Chain
YO = yarn over
st = stitch
beg = beginning
sl st = Slip stitch
sc = Single Crochet
dc = Double Crochet
(B) = reminder that this row uses beads
b in front of stitch name = beads are included in that stitch
blp = Bead Loop. When more than one bead is included before doing a YO, a number will indicate how many beads should be pulled up to form the loop.

refer to *www.learntocrochet.com* for more information

STRING: 2 yards of size 11° beads on main thread.
INSTRUCTIONS:
You will be working in rounds from the inside of the bag, starting at the bottom and working up to the top cuff. You will then add the drawstring and necklace.

Add a bead (bsc): Put the hook in the next stitch and advance the next bead. Snug it right next to your crochet work. Yarn over past the bead and make the next yarn over as usual.

• **Beaded Loop (sc with 40 blp):** Put the hook in the next stitch and advance the number of beads indicated (40). Snug them up to your crochet work. Yarn over past the bead loop and make the next yarn over as usual.

CONSTRUCTION:
Begin: Carry main thread and metallic thread as if they are one.
• **Rnd 1:** Chain 6 and join with a Slip stitch to form a circle. • **Rnd 2**(B): Ch1. Repeat the following pattern 6 times: 1 sc with 40 blp and 1 sc in the next stitch. When repeats are complete, join to beginning ch with sl st (12 st, 6 blps). • **Rnd 3**(B): Ch 1. Repeat the following pattern 12 times: 1 sc with 30 blp and 1 sc with 15 blp in the next stitch. When repeats are complete, join to beginning ch with sl st (24 blps). • **Rnd 4**(B): Ch 1. Repeat the following pattern 24 times: 1 sc with 20 blp in the next stitch. When repeats are complete, join to beginning ch with sl st (24 blps). • **Rnd 5**: Ch 3. Dc in same st. Repeat the following pattern 24 times: dc twice in the next stitch. When repeats are complete, join to beginning ch 3 with sl st (48 st). • **Rnd 6**: Ch 3. Repeat the following pattern 48 times: dc in the next stitch. When repeats are complete, join to beginning ch 3 with sl st (48 st). • **Rnd 7**: Ch 1. Repeat the following pattern 47 times: 1 sc in the next

continued on page 29

stitch. When repeats are complete, join to beginning ch with sl st (48 st). • **Rnd 8**(B): Ch 1. Repeat the following pattern 48 times: 1 sc with 3 blp in the next stitch. When repeats are complete, join to beginning ch with sl st (48 blps). • **Rnd 9**(B): Ch 1. Repeat the following pattern 48 times: 1 sc with 5 blp in the next stitch. When repeats are complete, join to beginning ch with sl st (48 blps). • **Rnd 10**(B): Ch 1. Repeat the following pattern 48 times: 1 sc with 7 blp in the next stitch. When repeats are complete, join to beginning ch with sl st (48 blps). • **Rnd 11**: Ch 1. Repeat the following pattern 48 times: 1 sc in the next stitch. When repeats are complete, join to beginning ch with sl st (48 st). • **Rnd 12**(B): Ch 1. Repeat the following pattern 24 times: bch 4, skip 1 st, 1 sc in the next stitch. When repeats are complete, join to sl st to first bch (24 bchs). • **Rnd 13**(B): Repeat the following pattern 24 times: bch 4, 1 sc between second and third bch of previous bch 4 round. When repeats are complete, join to first bch between second and third bch

(24 bchs). • **Rnd 14 and 15**(B): repeat row 13. • **Rnd 16**: Repeat the following pattern 24 times: Ch 1, 1 sc in the next stitch. (24 st). • **Rnd 17**: Repeat the following pattern 24 times: 1 dc. Join to first dc (24 dc). • **Rnd 18**: sc 24 times, join (24 sc). • **Rnd 19 and 20**: repeat row 18. • **Rnd 21**(B): Ch 1. Repeat the following pattern 24 times: 1 sc with 3 blp in next st. When repeats are complete, join to beginning ch with sl st (24 blps). • **Rnd 22**(B): Ch 1. Repeat the following pattern 24 times: 1 sc with 5 blp in next st. When repeats are complete, join to beginning ch with sl st (24 blps). • **Rnd 23**: sc 24 times. Join (24 sc). • **Rnd 24**: dc 24 times. Join (24 dc). • **Rnd 25**(B): Ch 1. Repeat the following pattern 24 times: 1 sc with 15 blp. Join (24 blp). • **Rnd 26**(B): Ch 1. Repeat the following pattern 24 times: 1 sc with 10 blp. Join (24 blp). • End.

Drawstring and necklace are continued on the next page.

This bag is crocheted using basic techniques. The beadwork is incorporated into the fabric creation rather than embellished onto a crocheted piece. This technique can be used for amulet bags, purses, ornaments, trimmed scarves and clothing. Anything that can be crocheted can be beaded with this technique.

the amulet mystique

by Laurel Kubby

To finish this amulet, insert good wishes and happy thoughts into your bag before pulling the drawstring shut. Enjoy wearing your one-of-a-kind creation.

continued from page 29

Crocheted Amulet Necklace & Drawstring

NECKLACE:
Using doubled beading thread, string 3 strands of size 11° beads. Add random size 8° beads, crystals, and gemstones for a more interesting look. Be sure the strands fit over your head loosely. Consider the finished length you want. Close the strands or put a clasp on them. Use a Lark's Head Knot to attach the necklace to the donut.

Tip: There are 2 options for making the drawstring. Option 1 is easier to pass through the neck of the bag and is more functional if you plan to put things into your bag. Option 2 is more attractive, but it is not as easy to open and close because the beads catch on the crocheted fabric.

DRAWSTRING:
Option 1: Work the main thread and metallic thread as one. Make a tight chain 12"-14" long. Using your crochet hook, pull it through the neck of the crochet bag, going outside to inside, every third stitch. Continue until you have completely circled the neck of the bag. • Using the drawstring, place a Lark's Head Knot through the stone donut. Tie the 2 ends of the drawstring together and work the knot into the bag so it won't show.
Option 2: String 18" of size 11° beads on the main thread. Work the main thread and metallic thread as one. Make a tight chain for $1\frac{1}{2}$"-2". Pull up 2-3 beads in each chain. Continue until the total strand is 10"-12" long. Continue making the tight chain without beads for $1\frac{1}{2}$"-2" more. Using your crochet hook, pull it through the neck of the bag, going outside to inside, every 3 stitches. • Using the drawstring, place a Lark's Head Knot through the stone donut. Tie the two ends of the drawstring together and work the knot into the bag so it won't show.

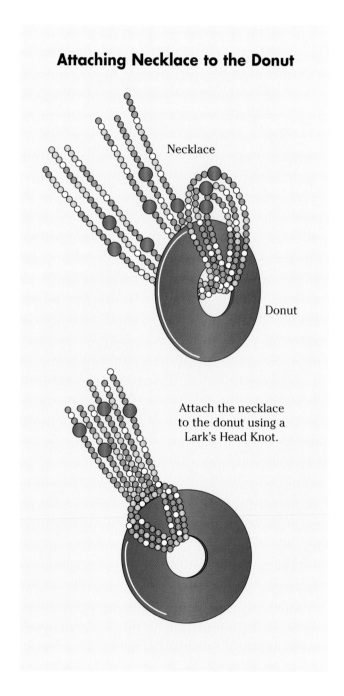

Attaching Necklace to the Donut

Necklace

Donut

Attach the necklace to the donut using a Lark's Head Knot.

"The donut necklace may be worn with or without the amulet bag, an added plus."

– Laurel Kubby

Adding the Drawstring to the Amulet Bag

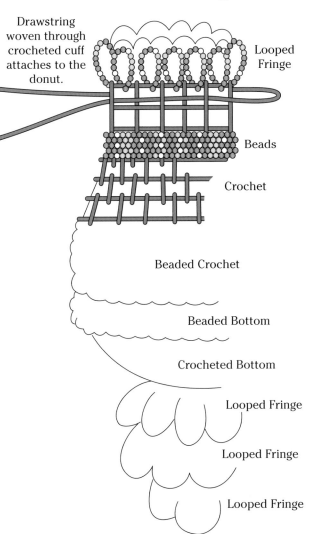

Drawstring woven through crocheted cuff attaches to the donut.

Looped Fringe

Beads

Crochet

Beaded Crochet

Beaded Bottom

Crocheted Bottom

Looped Fringe

Looped Fringe

Looped Fringe

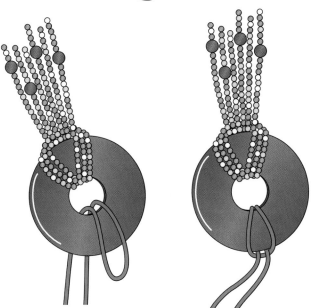

The drawstring for the amulet bag is attached to the donut using a Lark's Head Knot.

66 Lavish bead crochet emerged in the early 1800's along with other forms of elaborate needlework. However, bead crochet first appeared on the market in the 1830's. 99

– Mary Libby Neiman

smooth operator

Easy

For those who like organic art, this rope necklace has the look and feel of polished river stones. The beads chosen for this project have a natural sheen, and the rope has both weight and substance.

Bead Crocheted Rope

handmade focal beads and rope by
Karen Ovington, contact her at 773-764-5200

MATERIALS: 1 spool Conso upholstery thread • Beads (130 grams of size 6° seeds, 1 or more hand-made glass focal beads) • Steel 1.5mm hook • #20 tapestry needle • Hypo Cement

STRING:
All beads on the thread. Leave thread attached to the spool, do not cut.

CONSTRUCTION:
Make 6 Bead-Chain stitches with a 12" tail and join in a beaded circle. • Make a Bead-Slip stitch in each stitch. Continue until tube measures length desired. Tube shown is 37" long. • In the last row, Slip stitch 6 stitches without a bead. Leave hook in last loop, expand size of loop to pass spool through, remove hook and tighten loop. Cut, leaving a 16" tail.

Place glass lampwork beads on longer thread and pass the other thread through. Pull both threads until both ends of rope butt tightly against the lamp-work beads. • Thread 1 tail through a needle and push needle up through the center of the rope 1", and out through the side of the rope, making sure not to exit through a bead hole.

Put needle back into the rope, 1 stitch away from where the thread exited. Push needle back to the bottom of the rope. Make a stitch through the thread at the bottom of the rope, leaving a loop and then stitching through the loop. Knot again and tight-en firmly. Glue. Let dry and trim.

Repeat with the thread on the other side.

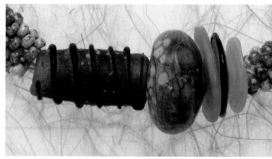

star treatment

Dark green ivy mixes well with bright red for a bracelet reminiscent of holly berries at Christmas. If you are looking for a more subtle, dainty project, check out the very feminine pastel flowering vine.

Berries in the Ivy

by Mary Libby Neiman

MATERIALS: 8 yards *On the Surface* New Metallic thread • Beads (8 faceted 4mm Red crystals, 64 size 8° Red seed, 108 size 8 hex cut Silver-lined Green, 924 size 11° Black seed) • Steel 1.25 - 1.4 mm hook • Needles (#24 tapestry and #10 beading) • Hypo Cement • Clasp

STRING:

1ST SECTION: 4 size 11° seeds, 1 size 8 hex, 5 size 11° seeds, 1 size 8 hex * 5 size 11° seeds, 1 size 8 hex. Repeat from * 10 more times.

NEXT 8 SECTIONS: 3 size 8° seeds, 3 size 11° seeds, 1 size 8° seed, 1 crystal, 1 size 8 hex * 5 size 11° seeds, 1 size 8 hex. Repeat from * 11 more times.

If you need a larger bracelet, add one or more sections.

CONSTRUCTION:

Make 6 Bead-Chain stitches. Join into a circle. • Make a Bead-Slip stitch every stitch until all beads are crocheted and tube measures 8".

CLASP FINISH:

To add a clasp, place loop end of one half of the clasp into the center of the bead crochet tube. Sew back and forth through the hole several times until the clasp is firmly attached. Stitch your thread into the tube, exiting several rows from the end. Apply a small amount of clear glue and trim thread. • Repeat on the other end with the other half of the clasp.

JOIN FINISH:

To join the ends now, check to see that the joined bracelet will slide over your hand. This is the time to add one or more complete repeats of beads. • Leave hook in last loop to hold it open. Cut thread leaving a 12" tail. Pull cut end of tail through the last loop, remove crochet hook and tighten loop. Thread tail through a needle. • Join your ends together by stitching first from last hex bead on one end to the last hex bead on the other end. Continue stitching, matching beads and keeping stitches pulled tight to avoid gaps in the join. Thread 12" tail into needle and stitch from one end to the other twice. Bury and glue both tails in the tube. Let dry and trim.

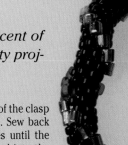

Pastels Flowering Vine

by Mary Libby Neiman

Tip: If you are going to use a clasp, you may wish to thread these extra beads to make the first and last flower the same distance from the clasp: 5 size 11° seeds, 1 size 8 hex. • Repeat 10 times.

MATERIALS: 8 yards *On the Surface* New Metallic thread • Beads (8 faceted 4mm Yellow crystal, 64 size 8° Mauve seed, 108 size 8 AB Green hex cut, 924 size 11° White seed) • Steel 1.25 - 1.4 mm hook • Needle (#24 tapestry or #10 beading) • Hypo Cement • Optional clasp

STRING:

1st Section: 4 size 11° seeds, 1 size 8 hex, 5 size 11° seeds, 1 size 8 hex. * 5 size 11° seeds, 1 size 8 hex. Repeat from * 5 more times.

Next 8 Sections: 3 size 8° seeds, 3 size 11° seeds, 1 size 8° seed, 1 crystal, 1 size 8 hex * 5 size 11° seeds, 1 size 8 hex. Repeat from * 11 more times.

Last Section: 5 size 11° seeds, 1 size 8 hex. Repeat 5 times.

If you need a larger bracelet, add one or more repeats of the pattern.

CONSTRUCTION:

Make 6 Bead-Chain stitches. Join into a circle. • Make a Bead-Slip stitch every stitch until all beads are crocheted and tube measures 8".

Clasp finish: To add a clasp, place loop end of one half of the clasp into the center of the bead crochet tube. Sew back and forth through the hole several times until the clasp is firmly attached. Stitch your thread into the tube, exiting several rows from the end. Apply a small amount of clear glue and trim thread. • Repeat on the other end with the other half of the clasp.

Join finish: To join the ends now, check to see that the joined bracelet will slide over your hand. This is the time to add one or more complete repeats of beads. • Leave hook in last loop to hold it open. Cut thread leaving a 12" tail. Pull cut end of tail through the last loop, remove crochet hook and tighten loop. Thread tail through a needle. • Join your ends together by stitching first from last hex bead on one end to the last hex bead on the other end. Continue stitching, matching beads and keeping stitches pulled tight to avoid gaps in the join. Thread 12" tail into needle and stitch from one end to the other twice. Bury and glue both tails in the tube. Let dry and trim.

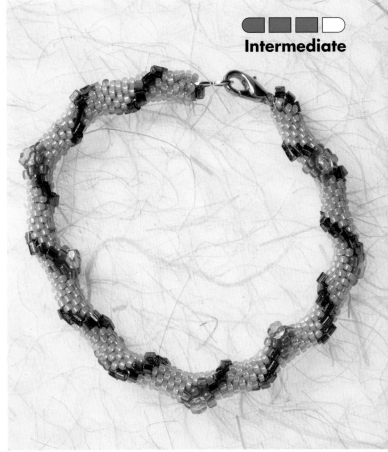

crochet's hottest trends

Where To Buy

SUPPLIERS - Most craft and variety stores carry an excellent assortment of supplies. If you need something special, ask your local store to contact the following companies:

BEADS
> Caravan Beads, 800-230-8941, Portland, ME
> Helby Import, 732-969-5300, Carteret, NJ
> Tambrook Bead, 503-235-2282, Portland, OR

JOHN JAMES TAPESTRY AND BEADING NEEDLES
> Colonial Needle, 914-946-7474, White Plains, NY
> Helby Import, 732-969-5300, Carteret, NJ

BATES STEEL CROCHET HOOKS
> Coats and Clark, 800-241-5997, Greer, SC

BOYE STEEL CROCHET HOOKS
> Wrights, 800-628-9362, Warren, MA

ANCHOR THREAD
> Coats and Clark, 800-241-5997, Greer, SC

CONSO NYLON BEADING THREAD
> Helby Import, 732-969-5300, Carteret, NJ

NEW METALLIC THREAD
> On the Surface, 847-675-2520, Wilmette, IL

PEARL COTTON
> DMC, 973-589-0606, S. Kearny, NJ

SILK THREAD
> Gudebrod Inc, 610-327-4050, Pottstown, PA
> YLI, 803-985-3100, Rock Hill, SC

HYPO CEMENT
> Helby Import, 732-969-5300, Carteret, NJ

MANY THANKS to my friends
for their cheerful help
and wonderful ideas!
Kathy McMillan • Jennifer Laughlin
Patty Williams • Marti Wyble
Janie Ray • Donna Kinsey
David & Donna Thomason

Meet the Designers

Mary Libby Neiman

Mary Libby is a fiber and bead-work designer. Her beautiful and original work has appeared in BEADWORK *maga-zine, in* DESIGN ORIGINALS *books and on the Carol Duvall TV Show.*

Designing 'New Metallic' thread for her fibers company, **On the Surface**, *led her to bead crochet. She is very excited about focusing on new techniques for working with fibers and beads.*

Laurel Kubby

Laurel really enjoys designing and teach-ing beadwork and making custom bead-ed jewelry. Her work can be seen in sever-al magazines and books, including BEADWORK, LAPIDARY JOURNAL, STEP BY STEP BEADS, *and* BEADING WITH HERRINGBONE STITCH.

Janet Ohle

Although crochet is her main fiber art, Janet is also an accomplished hand spinner with awards for her hand spun yarn. She is active the the creative arts community, and is cur-rently the Vice President for the Northern Illinois Chapter of the Crochet Guild of America.

Gwen Blakley Kinsler

Founder of the Crochet Guild of America, Gwen is in the forefront of the hottest new tech-niques as she teaches nationally. Author of the new book, KIDS CAN DO IT CROCHETING, *her designs have been included in* BEAD & BUTTON, BEADWORK, ARTS & CRAFTS, *and* PIECEWORK.

Karen Ovington

Karen is the owner of a handmade glass beads business called **Ovington Glass Studio**. *As a nationally renowned beadmaker, her beads and bead crochet have been featured in numerous bead magazines and books, including the cover of* BEAD & BUTTON.